Poems from the Heart

Second Edition

Poems from the Heart

SECOND EDITION

Written By

PETER BENJAMIN LEBUHN

Order this book online at www.trafford.com
or email orders@trafford.com

Most Trafford titles are also available at major online book retailers.

Printed in the United States of America.

ISBN: 978-1-4269-5064-3 (sc)
ISBN: 978-1-4269-5065-0 (e)

Trafford rev. 11/29/2010

www.trafford.com

North America & international
toll-free: 1 888 232 4444 (USA & Canada)
phone: 250 383 6864 • fax: 812 355 4082

GROWING UP IN THE LATE 1960'S AND 1970'S, MY MUSICAL ,AND POETIC INFLUENCES WERE VAN MORRISON,THE BEATLES AND THE MAMAS AND THE PAPAS. NOW, A LOCAL WRITER IN THE PHILADELPHIA AREA. MANY WORDS THAT ARE WRITTEN AND SPOKEN ARE FROM REAL LIFE AND FEELING. THIS IS WHAT I ATTEMPT TO CONVEY TO THE READER AS I WRITE, TO PULL THE READER INTO THE EXPERIENCE AS I WRITE. MANY OF MY WRITINGS ARE SPIRTUAL AND ROMANTIC IN NATURE. THEY ARE ALL WRITTEN FROM THE HEART MY WAY OF SHARING WITH ALL OF YOU WHO I AM.

IF YOU WOULD LIKE TO REACH ME MY BUSINESS PAGE IS WWW.PETERLEBUHN.COM

MY POETRY PAGE IS WWW.PETERLEBUHNWRITINGS.COM

WRITING POETRY SINCE 1983, I HAVE BEEN ABLE TO EXPRESS MY EMOTIONS FROM SPRITUAL, ROMANTIC ,EXOTIC AND TIGER POEMS THAT I WROTE FOR A SAVE THE TIGER CAMPAIGN IN NEPAL FOR ARCHANA SHRESTA, A GOOD FRIEND.

ALL OF THESE WRITINGS CAME FROM MY HEART THEY ARE TRULY "POEMS FROM THE HEART"

I Dedicate this book to all lovers of the written word and poetry and I hope these words speak to your life

Peter Benjamin LeBuhn

CONTENTS

Las Alturas Del Amor....xi

A Love Song....1
A Second Chance....3
All That Was Hidden...All To Be Shown....4
An Epic Kiss....5
As A Lioness To Her Pray....7
Be Encouraged....9
Beacon Of Light....10
Beacon Of Light (Spanish)....12
Beautiful Thief....14
Beautiful Thief Returns....16
Beautiful Thief Triology....18
Beautiful Thief ,Glowing Hearts....20
Breathless....21
Brought Alive....23
Burning Desire....24
Butterfly....26
Gentle Kisses, Butterfly Light....28
Chambre Of Desire....30
Coursing Passion....32
Court Of Love....33
Desire....35
Dancing Panthers(A Love Story)....37
Dark Forests....39
Delicato!!!Delicato!!!....40
Destiny....42
Do You Like What You See....43
Dreams, What Greatness Is Made Of!....45
Duece Game....47
The Voice On The Radio....49
En Paris Ces't Ma Maison....50

Encapsulated 52
Erotic Explorations 54
Exploring A Mystery 56
Fire And Water 58
Fountain Of Passion 60
French Maidens Of The Sea 62
Fruits,Flowers,Satin Sheets 64
God, I Am Hot 65
Grace And Honor 67
Greatness 69
Guilty Pleasure 70
Happenstance 71
Harvest Fantasy 73
Hold On 75
I Knew It When I Saw Your Face 77
In The GrooVe Of The Night 79
In The Hush Calm Of The Twilight 80
In Your Eyes 83
Juicy Necter, Wet Lips 84
Jungle Love 86
Kiss Of A Lover 88
La Belle De Le Terre 90
Last Days 91
Last Of The Golden Boyz 92
Le Tigre Puissant 94
Live Wire 95
Lonely In The Night 97
Love 99
Love At First Sight 100
Love In Many Languages 102
Love,Holy Cow 103
Loves Maiden Voyage 105
Lyric Of A Love Song 107
Lyrical Verses 109
Maidens Of The Sea (French) 110
Midnight Hour 111
Midnight Juices 113
Mighty Tiger 116
Molten Love 117

Monday FlowErs 119
Music Hall Funk 121
My Angel 123
My China Rose 124
My First Love 125
My Latina Rose (Spanish) 127
My Potion 128
Nature In All Her Flavor 130
Oh What A World!!! 132
Ojos Españoles 134
Olde Glories...New Promises 135
Our Hearts Uncharted 136
Paris I Adorent 138
Paris It Is My Home (French) 139
Passion Into Action 140
Peacea Poem Written In 75 Minutes On A Trip To Baltimore, Md.... 141
Peace In A Hectic World 142
Penetrating Love 144
Peter Lebuhn: A Biography 148
Pleasures Of Thy Heart 150
Première Passion(French) 152
Puerto Rico 154
Rhythm Of The Night 155
Sexual Fire From Within 157
Silence 159
Silently Naked 160
Sing A New Song 163
Slice Of Time 165
Slow Sex 167
So Hot, So Passionate 169
Solving For The Unknown 170
Spanish Eyes 171
Storybook Memories Of Puerto Rico(Spanish) 173
The Beaver 174
The Call 175
The Dance 177
The Exotic Eternal Dance 178
The Expressionless Page 180
Thy Faithful Servant 181

The Feast 183
The Forbidden Kiss 185
The Gift Of Life 187
Heights Of Love 188
The Invinceable Tiger 190
The Journey 191
The Key To Your Heart 192
The Kiss 193
The Living Song 195
The Magic Of Love In The Moonlight 196
The Ones That Got Away...The One That Stayed!!! 198
The Open Door 199
The Quiteness Of My Heart 200
The Spirit Within 201
The Tapestry Of Who We Are 202
The Teacher 204
The Vessel 205
The Tigress (Lonely In The Night) 206
Theatre De Amour 208
Theatre Of The Unknown 209
These Dreams 210
Thoughts Of You Wrap Around My Soul 212
Timeless 213
To Serve 214
To The White Sea 215
Transport To Ecstasy 216
Un BeSo Epico(A Spanish Crossover Song) 218
Unbridled Love 221
Waiting 222
We Will Love Again 224
When Night Becomes Day 226
Without Word 228
Wondrous Life 230
Your Golden Kiss 231
Touch Me There 233
Your Touch Means So Much 234

LAS ALTURAS DEL AMOR

Las Alturas del Amor tartan frotar ligeramente con suavidad sensuous
que disimula
Vener antes del thee pelado, abierto y crudo. Sus manos apacibles
resbalan
A traves y tragin mi cuerpo en el movimiento del tendor. Por
Segundo...ir
mas rapido
Como una locomocion del vapor. Agarrado por sus manos exible suaves
que me
Toman profundamente...en su garganta densamente en su cuerpo que
palpita
Rhythmically, stronghold que pulsa sobre mi eje. Esto es verdad un arte
de
Placer. Abundante con su es _______________ mulo de thy del
fella _______________ o toma a thee mas
Arriba mi aceleracion del Corazon, volando en la passion deliciosa
Ejaculate sobre su paladar sensual y machihiembrele expreso su
Placer como incorporamos una passion de ninguna vuelta. La sensacion
Que desconcierta, agradando. Usted que prueba mi pocion del amor con
toda su emocion...

La sed de Hmmmmmmmmmmmmmmmmm...Ohhh I, anhela, desea

para

usted

Mas lejos mientras que nuestro

a

---

aire aguanta. Usted me ha traido a

las Alturas del amor

Que usted me ha traido a las Alturas del amor.

A LOVE SONG

Oh, I met you one late July afternoon
Your silhouette glistening
Oh, the radiance of the sun.
Time spent in the back of an 'Ol
Light Blue Olds
Never to Forget
The carnal sweat
You look at me
Your eyes began to SWOON!!!
With desire
Your hearts on FIRE!!!
Oh, that one day late in July
That one afternoon
Time spent in the back of an 'Ol
Light Blue Olds
The carnal sweat
Telling you of the dreams of you
A dream of you and I walking hand In hand
beneath
The MOON!!!
And now you tell

You tell me...I tell you
I love you
Isn't it strange how lovers start as friends?
(Slow Talk)Now there's something I got to tell you
Something that can only be written down
Now every time I am around you Babe
(Every time I am around you)
There is magic in the air
A feeling of taking flight
Oh, so high in the sky
And now you tell me,
You tell me...I tell you
I love you
Now we know this love is true

A SECOND CHANCE

A second chance
To Dance
To Live...To Sing...To Be Thankful
And Give
I set apart this opulent opportunity
Not for myself
For I am put on the shelf
A second chance to serve
With a narrow faith
Ne'er to swerve
Once Fallen
Broken Wings
Now I understand to serve my King
All of my Heart
All of my Mind
All of my Soul
...A Second Chance
...A Second Chance

ALL THAT WAS HIDDEN…ALL TO BE SHOWN

I come before thee
Naked
Bearing myself to you
with all of my soul to see
All that was hidden
All to be shown
It seems such a crime
Not to let it be known

Appearing before your glory
Blinded by your presence
and mastery

I come humbled before you
Lifted up on wings of eagles
You raise me.
Your grace…Your mercy
saves me
All that was hidden..All to be shown

Peter B LeBuhn

AN EPIC KISS

An Epic KISS
Helpless in your rhapsody
The sweet discovery found
Under your body
Lost in your abyss
Lost in your arms…Your legs wrapped around Thee
There is no place I would rather be.
Dripping in Passionate Sweat
Stunning is your silhouette.
Osculating, caressing
Our love confessing.
'Neath the MOON
The STARS
Alone in nature…It is ours.
To see your glow
It does show
Your happiness
As you lay in mine arms.
Setting off my sexual alarms.
Taken Higher
…Thy Body Sexually set on fire

My heart flaming and aroused
As you present yourself with sexual invitation
Your sweet flavor…I savor
Smell of Strawberries… Chocolate
Inside your deep Chinese Body
Throbbing, Pulsating
Rhythm in LOVE
You Have Thee with your Epic Kiss
…Your Epic KISS

AS A LIONESS TO HER PRAY

Dripping in Heat
Sweat rolling of my Cheek
With your greet
My heart beats, Higher, HIGHER

Before you I stand
Breathless
Wanting More

You stand 'fore me
We are like two sex savages
Poised for attack
I want you...I want...you...I WANT YOU
All your sweat...Vigor...discharged
You leap across on me
Tasting me...As a lioness to Her prey
Licking every inch of your prize
Lying Spread Eagle on the Bed

Feeling...

...Watching You

Give Me Head.

Peter LeBuhn

BE ENCOURAGED

Be encouraged
Consider everything in every nature
A gift
Humble thyself
Not Displacing importance of your ownself
Exalting others before you
In Death There is Life
Ne'er an end in sight
Though on earth beaten and ravaged
He shines as the stars
Living in One Nations Hearts
In The End
Every knee bows
Every tongue confesses
You are the One True God
And Jesus Christ
Lord and Savior
Amen

Peter LeBuhn

BEACON OF LIGHT

You are my beacon of light
Your illumination lights my path
The trail I walk
The course I take
Unknown
My heart IS
Filled with Your Love
And Treasure for Creation
Your teachings are my Nation
Your ways Incarnation

My Beacon of Light
I have no Fright
You have made the darkness
Bright

One Scripture...One Christ

One Word...One God

ONE GLORY

The Five Solas

Forever Ring True

BEACON OF LIGHT (SPANISH)

You are my Beacon of Light
(Usted es mi faro de la luz)
Your illumination lights my path
(Su iluminación enciende mi trayectoria)
The trial I walk
(El rastro camino)
The course I take
(El curso que tomo)
Unknown
(Desconocido)
My heart IS
Filled with Your Love
(Mi corazón se llena de su amor)
And Treasure for Creation
Your teachings are my Nation
Your ways Incarnation
(Y el tesoro para la creación sus enseñanzas es mi nación su encarnación de las maneras)
My Beacon of Light
I have no Fright
(Mi faro de la luz no tengo ningún fright)

You have made the darkness

Bright

(Usted ha hecho la oscuridad brillante)

One Scripture...One Christ

One Word...One God

ONE GLORY

The Five Solas

Forever Ring True

(Un Scripture... Una Palabra De Cristo Uno... Una GLORIA Del Dios UNO

Los Cinco Solas Suena Por siempre Verdad)

Peter LeBuhn

BEAUTIFUL THIEF

ALL POEMS IN THE BEAUTIFUL THIEF SERIES ARE DEDICATED TO CATHY DELU WHO INSPIRED THEM

A beauty in the far off mist
Appearing to me for a tryst
On this night of nights
The moon shines bright
You enter as a thief
through the smoldering fog

Enter you do bit by bit
mesmerized as to what is to
come next.
Bits and pieces of you glowing
showing. Bits and pieces...Not

Long Flowing Hair Smooth as Silk
Coconut skin
Your arms and legs a sight to behold

You are the Thief that has stolen my heart
The Beautiful Thief that will not depart

Peter LeBuhn

BEAUTIFUL THIEF RETURNS

A cool breeze blows across my face
Left breathless in my space
It is The Beautiful Thief
...The one that stole my Heart
Thoughts that You were to depart
Now known that your affection is of
Essence.
Thine Eyes twinkle
Sparkling Like Diamonds
My Heart...A flutter...The Return
Of The Beautiful Thief.
You are The Pirate That Holds My Heart.
The cool breeze... Now A Strong Wind
Engulfing us Together
Fused in our Passions
The Fire Has Returned
The Flame Has Been Lit

The Fires of Our Hearts

...Reach The Sky

Return of The Beautiful Thief

Peter LeBuhn

BEAUTIFUL THIEF TRIOLOGY

The Fire between us blazing
What has ignited cannot be overcome
Our Passion Razing
Our Sensations Give Way To Temptation
Thy Beautiful Thief...You Are Back
The admission fee of this love...Free
Feel the vibration
'Neath The Full Moon
The Bright Stars
Smiling Upon Us
As we caress, confess and express
Our love
Living a Moment that many only dream of.
Smothered in your arms
Giving way to your charms.
Your sweet lips...Your hips
hold me in a passionate eclipse.
Gone You Were...Now Your Return

The Return of the Beautiful Thief

The Trilogy of the Beautiful Thief

...The future is Ours to Take

...The future is Ours to Make,

Peter LeBuhn

BEAUTIFUL THIEF ,GLOWING HEARTS

Gratifying hearts emitting passion and sexual desire
Radiant eyes transfixed, two on two
The Thief Beautiful Is She has stolen me
Once Again
Magnetic lust, gravitational yearning
Connecting souls
Flowing desires
Luscious, juicy, tongues dancing
Both of us bottomless, Deep inside loves sweet flavor
Uncontrollable, bursting
Oh Beautiful Thief
Flesh on Flesh, writhing bodies
Torrid Heat, fire, burning desires
Tasting, teasing, tantalizing
Licking, dripping, flaming
Energy, orbiting, culminating
Driven, synergistic, Pure X-T-C

Peter LeBuhn

BREATHLESS

breathless, clutching, writhing
You take thee
twisting, jerking, bucking
Alive you are riding me
Exploding your senses
You are Free
One...I In you
You in me
Intertwined, conjoined
Forever in this moment
Ne'er to end...a moment frozen
Yet moving in time
For you
Available to fall
Again and again
eternally
internally

passionate, intrinsic, animalistic
returning to connectedness
with my body
proof of exertion
yet relieved of tension
flows like the tide
upon my psyche

2006 Peter LeBuhn

BROUGHT ALIVE

Brought Alive by your beauty
To love you...My Duty
It is Just You and I
Your love you Supply

The walk down Chestnut Street
Makes me Feel Complete
Through the Campus our walk
As it goes from block to block

Hand in hand
Arm in Arm
In the Moment With You
You with me

These are the things memories are made of
These are the things memories are made of

Peter LeBuhn

BURNING DESIRE

Breathing deeply, slowly
QUICKLY
Closing my eyes
Feeling your softness as I enter you
At first your face
Your Image running through my mind
Finding the dark corners and filling them with light
Flowing through into my mouth and dancing across my tongue
Letting my taste buds devour your exotic flavour
You pour swiftly into my heart, into my soul
Warming me from the inside out
Touching, caressing me with wave after wave of desire
You are taking me higher
We speak of love
A hunger....
Show me what you hunger
Let me bring out your tiger
Let me smell your arousal
Tempting thee with wandering hands
My throbbing desire pushing, grinding
Faster, madder, deeper

Loves sweet pleasure-pain
You beg for me to touch you
Take you to that place only you and I can go
So you may drown in the beauty of it
Your groans of delight urge me to try harder
You plead with me not to stop, you are almost there
And then you give yourself fully unto me
Rise and crest over and into our world
Our ticket to get here
Unfaltering trust

Peter LeBuhn 2006

BUTTERFLY

Like a Butterfly
You rest on the evening star
...Where you are resting afar
This song which holds our spirits kindrid
Live From Day to Night

Many Struggles...
Tears
Embraces
The joy of something grand
A cultivated harmonious friendship
...With No Limits
...You A friend without blemish
...You stole my heart
Now I must make my stand
...These dreams
...These thoughts of you

Unexplainable

What say you of me?

My precious butterfly

...Don't fly far

...Don't fly far

Peter LeBuhn

Peter LeBuhn

Peter LeBuhn

GENTLE KISSES, BUTTERFLY LIGHT

Gentle kisses
Butterfly light,
Not all I desire,
This dark, stormy night.

Let Go...Let Go
Let your passions take over
Let Go...Let Go
Throwing myself at you...Yourself at Me
With a growl like a huntress from the Jungle!

Feeling me as I enter,
Carnal lust,
Sensual pleasure
Crying out with
Every forceful thrust!

'I love you'
'I want you'
'I must have you'

Feeling my lightning Rod,
Hearing the thunder deep inside,
The floodgates of passion open,
Nothing to hide!

Thoughts of only you cross thy mind
This electric stormy night,
Succumbing to your Butterfly kisses,
Your touch by.. Butterfly light!

2006 Peter LeBuhn

CHAMBRE OF DESIRE

I see you from afar
In the faint mist of the night
My passions are at the highest
of heights
Burning...Yearning
After you
I call your name
and you look my way
Come here
Come into my world
Enter into my chambre of desire
Explore the Fires
That burn from within
Light a match to your passions
Burn out of control
Let your body take control
The pleasure you will feel

From head to toe

Melting...Melting into the fold

of my body becoming ONE

Peter B LeBuhn

COURSING PASSION

You take me
Thy body yours
to take
Passion...Rushing...Coursing
Through Our Veins
Encapsulated by your scent
you were Heaven Sent
A Prisoner of Love
Given to me by the Stars Above
The Fateful Words Uttered
I Love You
The same come in return
Thy heart has begun to burn
Thy heart has begun to yearn

Peter LeBuhn

COURT OF LOVE

An Anniversary Song
Answers In A Game Of Questions
After The Sensations
The Midnight Hour
Increases Thy Power
...Thy Love Heightened from above
Coming before thee
...Naked...Bare...Raw
In your Court of Love
...Found Guilty
You sentence thee
To a lifetime of passion

By The River

...We Go

A care ne'er to take

Our love we partake

An Anniversary Song

Forever to be sung

Peter LeBuhn

DESIRE

All your desires
Uncensored intense passion of emotion
savage sexual abandonment
At first glance
Unrestraint of Passions
Come, taste me
Ripe, sweet body of lust
Nectar made of me
A gift to quench your thirst

Liquid love dripping off my carnal body
Our sex...As we are engulfed
To be savored
By the touch of your lips
The caress of your tongue

Come, love me
Pure undeniable longing
To have my body taken
Made one with yours

Posses me like no other

Enter my soul

Fill me with yourself

Ecstasy awaits us

Peter LeBuhn

Dancing Panthers(A Love Story)

You come upon thee
Dancing slowly
Akin to the theater in the round
Your smile on passionate ground
Mischievous as a pirate to her prey.

Circling 'round each other
As Black Panthers
Atop A Hill Of Green
Hoping to unveil the things
Unseen.

The Sun Beats down
On Our bare backs
Your breasts...Inviting
This situation... exciting...delighting

The Heat Rises

In Store Many Surprises

Back on your rear feet are you

Pouncing on your lover...your prey

To your love I am bay

Your Samson Am I
My Delilah Are You

Peter LeBuhn

DARK FORESTS

Dark forests...Northern...Southern Mountains,
Fierce tigers circle around the villages in broad daylight.
...To The red dawn of twilight
The skies shine bright
Protecting what is theirs
In the magic of the night
The tigers roam everywhere taking lives for food.
The Majesty of the tigers power,
The prey dare not make a sound.
The new kin tiger sprout every year
In the valleys low.
Male and female tigers come up and down the mountains in large groups.
There is a village near the tigers' dens in the valley,
Where tigers often come and eat the villagers' brown calves.
Rich young men dare not shoot the arrows at the tigers.
The Majesty of the Tiger lives forever
The Majesty of the Tiger
They only pretend to check for the tigers' tracks in the forests.

Peter LeBuhn

DELICATO!!!DELICATO!!!

Delicato! ! ! Delicato! ! !
Delicious is Your Name.
In My Heart
The Flame Burns
And Speaks Delicato! ! ! Delicato! ! !
Delicious is your name
Take me to the point of no return
Generate and Deliver My Passions
...To the Highest of Heights
Bursting...Yearning
'Neath the Midnight Skies
As you look into mine eyes
Your thighs against me
Mine Against You
Thrusting...Desiring...Wanting
Delicatio! ! ! Delicato! ! !
Your Candy Kiss...A Deep Kiss

Reaches my Soul…As we embrace
Face to Face
Delicato! ! ! Delicato! ! ! I scream your name
Delicious is Your Name
Delicious is Your Name

Peter LeBuhn

DESTINY

Frightened Yet Excited
The Elixir of You
Draws me nearer...Closer
Wanting to Know more
Wanting to Run away.

The Unknown...Exciting
Exhilarating!
Every Piece of the Puzzle
Every Nuance of You
Makes me Want you more.

It is as if
WE control the Unknown
Control the future
...Our Destiny

Peter B LeBuhn

DO YOU LIKE WHAT YOU SEE

I am glad that you like what you see
But one thing I must tell you is that you can never like it too much.
Once you taste it, you will like it more and more.
I want you to picture this if you will
You coming home from work
The lights are dim
There is a white tablecloth on the table
Candles
and rose pedals on the rug
But the only thing is I am nowhere to be found: (
You look and look for me
Finally you find me
I am upstairs in the Bedroom
I stand before you
Naked, Bare, RAW
In all my glory for you to enjoy
I have come for your tasting pleasure
The dinner sits on the table
You want desert first
I have white wine and strawberries for you
Some chocolate too that you can eat off me

It is melted and hot
How erotic it sounds
We make love
Boy do we make love
Engulfing in each others passions
we have become one body
My Gentle touch surrounds you
as I kiss you and caress you
Your entire body in a shiver
All I want to do is make you quiver
Keep you coming back for more
Peter LeBuhn

DREAMS, WHAT GREATNESS IS MADE OF!

A thought
A dream
A glimmer of light that takes Flight
In the middle of the Night
These are the things of Greatness
For time is of the essence
There can be no lateness
To reach the pinnacle
The time for action
is now
Do Not Bow
Take your dream into action
For it is with a thought
A Dream
that great things are built on! !
Freedom: Built on A Dream
We have America

Electricity: Built on A Dream
We have Heat
Dreams What Greatness is made of
Thoughts into action what Greatness is made of!

Peter LeBuhn

DUECE GAME

THE NEXT TWO POEMS ARE FOR MY GOOD FRIEND CYNDY DRUE

Is it Advantage In?
Is it Advantage Out?
Or Deuce?
Many Questions surround my heart
Unsure of what has been entered into
I know what I see
It is good and blessed
The direction yet to be seen
Many Questions
remain not asked
dancing delicately
in and around conversations
In time you will know
So we will go
and grow

My heart that is softening
No more questions will it surround
The questions that need to be asked
Soon will no longer remain.
It will be a deuce game equal partnership

Peter B LeBuhn

THE VOICE ON THE RADIO

Your voice on the Radio
Touches my heart so
Your voice from afar
speaks to me so near

I smile as I listen
As I nervously glisten

My Name for all the world to hear
Is this the beginning
Of something dear

Peter B LeBuhn

En Paris Ces't Ma Maison

En Paris Ces't Ma Maison
The Paris Skylight
Shines upon your rose room in the early morning.
Portraits of the sea
portraits of Monet and Renoir...serene
boating scenes

You saunter to your full-length mirror
you comb your soft silky hair.
Joy is in your heart...You have found
Paradise.

Your morning walk begins
You pass the Luxemburg Gardens
Le Belle fleur de jar din
A smile glistens off your face
The Arc De Trimphe...The symbol of Liberties de France

The beauty continues
with the Champs Elysees
and the Concorde

In Paris you have found your heart
your love
your home

Peter LeBuhn

ENCAPSULATED

Encapsulated within my body,
Your back pressing against thy chest,
Bareness embedded in us
Stealing my manhood,
Laying aroused Silently as if to dream while awake
My heart to take
Your pulse keeping time with my heart.
Wondering where you are
Where this passion into action is taking you
Your awakening,
Taking you from behind,
Without care the alarm rings so early.
Then sweet surprise, you're stirring,
Sleepy fingers fondling,
In the wee hours of morning,
Feeding wanton hungering.
Desiring me as I sleep
Called into X-T- C
A fervor ...A shake
A Fount of love overflowing
Called forth to flow for your pleasure.

Side to back, head to foot,
Ampleness piercing entrance,
Intertwining like scissors,
We lock in a dance of ecstasy.
Hips thrusting thighs, clit reaching high,
Riding swelling waves,
I engulf you like a raging river,
Threatening to erupt floodgates.
Your passionate unrestraint
Opens my mind,
Loosing aching yearnings,
A secret longing fulfilled.
And flying free, my soul
Escapes these earthly confines,
Heaven bound,
To find itself delivered.

Peter LeBuhn

EROTIC EXPLORATIONS

Erotic Explorations
As you hold thee tight
In the midst of the Harvest Moon
I feel you...You Me
A Chalice of Burning Questions
Confessions and Desires Revealed
In Sweet Surrender
Pierced By Your Beauty
Our Hunger Grows
blossoming, flourishing
into the extraordinary
Taken Deep
In Loves Sweet Service
With You I feel Comfort
There is no Nervous

Sharing of our lives
as we thrive
To understand Love
The Respect
The Feeling

Peter LeBuhn

EXPLORING A MYSTERY

Your smile
Brings the warmth of the sun to my heart
When we are apart
It is you I think of in blissful memory
for the rest of my days.

Your hair unfurled
In golden locks of glorious disarray
As the sun shines upon you.

Your eyes inviting
As we frolic near the water stream
Nearer you come to me
Beaming
Shining
Your beauty Blinding

Blinding you may be I cannot help but be
Hypnotized by your captivating beauty
I must have you...My heart pounds like a
drum. Happiness has entered my life.

Peter LeBuhn

FIRE AND WATER

Wild Mountains
Cool Breeze
Wild Woman
Your Fire Powerful
My Waters just as strong
Will your Fire put out my waters
Will my Waters douse your flame
The challenge is yours to accept
Fire and Water
Two Passions...Powerful
when married as a force
Are you the one I am to explore
of the least of these?
The one who will understand my passions
and my actions.
Wild Woman
Fiery Woman

Let me douse your flame

Engulf yourself in my waters

Engulf yourself in my waters

Peter LeBuhn

FOUNTAIN OF PASSION

Lay your body next to mine
Let me feel the blazing heartbeat of you
Kissing Licking each other in the moist intimate of spots
tasting your passionate delicacy
The flavor to savor
the flavor from your erotic perfume
Breathing the aroma, fragrance of you
The sweet smells of your womanhood
Let me feel the desire, Take me higher
Hard and swollen, Plump between your thighs
You feast on me au naturel
Consume your hunger, your desire as you drink my fountain of passion
Come to me, Cum with me, I will show you X-T-C
Taken higher...to a land of desire
Our bodies quivering...trembling
Dripping whet in our Vibrations of Passion
Lost in Your body...Wrapped up
You have taken me home

You lost in my body

Your body is my home

Drenched in each others Passions

We have taken the action

Drenched in X-T-C

Drenched in X-T-C

Peter LeBuhn

FRENCH MAIDENS OF THE SEA

Remembrance of the beautiful green waves
And the sea tides tossing free
French maidens with sultry lips...and hips
Adorn the beauty and mystery of the ships
And the magic of the sea.
Love offshore
My French maidens
Given to me to love and adore.
In unison with the sound of the ocean roar
We come together rhythmically
With Pulsating love
The moon shines and smiles on us from above
The stars dance as we prance...Together
In unbridled love
On the deck of the ship our bodies engulfed
Lost in each others passions

French Maidens of the sea
One above me and two down below
French Maidens of the sea
with sultry lips...and hips
Your love hath adorned thee

Peter LeBuhn

FRUITS,FLOWERS,SATIN SHEETS

Fruits, Flowers,
Satin sheets
Branches of my heart
Beat for only One.
There is fear
Do not tear it with your hands,
Your beautiful eyes as they hypnotize
Your presence is soft.
It is not oft to meet such a prize.
Arriving morning dew
The wind comes to freeze thy face.
No matter... You are here with thee in this place.
Rest your silky feet..., Revel in these of moments dear
Your young centre let roll my sound
Toute head encor of your last kisses;
Let it calm down good storm,
And which I keep watch as you sleep and rest.

2006 Peter B. Lebuhn

GOD, I AM HOT

God. I'm hot.
My place is a mess
Sitting naked on my deck.
The moonlight...My clothing
As it shines off my body
The night air
The moon
The stars are such voyeurs
Thy wine glass drips wet beads of moisture
As you watch me
Dripping slowly running down
forming a wet circle
at the base of my
STRONG PECTORALS
to my navel
The journey about to begin
I spread my legs
You dive in
Sucking...Every last drop
of my pleasure craft
Thighs peeling apart

Head rolling back

Arms flying back

I gasp

God

I am Hot

God I am Hot

Peter LeBuhn

GRACE AND HONOR

To You I give Grace
To You I give Honor
For you are the one
...That has allowed me to save face

In trials and turmoil's
Troubles and Boils
You are there
In all of this universe
There is no compare

The One True
You make my soul Anew

To you True

Obedience is mine

I am yours

Your ways I will climb

Peter LeBuhn

GREATNESS

Greatness falls upon thee
as the rain showers to a stormy day.
Many storms...weathered
Many trials...sustained
Lives touched
My spirit becomes stronger
My testimony reaches further
with each individual
This Greatness is a gift
From the Father
He gave me talents
and told me to water and nurture them
The seeds have grown
To many in His name.
Thank you Father
for this Humble Greatness
Thank You.

Peter B LeBuhn

GUILTY PLEASURE

A smoke filled room
You appear in your masquerade costume
Music pumping
Feet thumping
People dancing...Bumping

The music heightens the excitement
I have fallen for you
Guilty Pleasure...
I am ready for the indictment

The future is now
MEOW...MEOW
To you I bow
Make my vow

This destiny is ours to make
This destiny ours to make

Peter LeBuhn

HAPPENSTANCE

Meeting by Happenstance
Our eyes
pulled together
It is as if we know each other
Drawing near to a kiss
Entering a world of never ending
BLISS
The Fantasy Has begun
Our songs of passion will be
SUNG
We are writing our own story into
HISTORY
Each moment...each second

It is precious

Our Hearts warm as the Sun

Cool as the Waters

What has Begun

Never to End! ! !

Never to End! ! !

Peter B LeBuhn

HARVEST FANTASY

The Day is dark
Rainy...and all so whet!
But with her
Life is illuminating
And warm

As we frolic in the rain
With all the passion and vigor
That our hearts can generate
Our arms wrapped around each other
With a tender embrace

The rain has ceased
The sun has risen
All the colors of the rainbow
Are upon us

As we lay in a mountain
Of colorful fall leaves

I look at her I know she is joyful
Because of the smile in her eyes
And the glow upon her face

Peter LeBuhn

HOLD ON

The moon shines bright
The stars overlooking above
On a clear night
We are separated afar

Do you think of me
Does your heart beat for thee
Hold On...Hold on Tight
To the One you Love.

Times of trial abound us
Temptations around
Hold On
Hold on Tight
You must believe what you have is true
Let's keep it simple

What we have will grow day by day

Week by Week Month by Month Year by Year

Hold On!

Hold On!

Peter LeBuhn

I KNEW IT WHEN I SAW YOUR FACE

I knew it when I saw your face
I don't know your name
It makes no difference just the same

Do you believe in Love at First Sight?
I hope and pray
You Will Say
'I just might'
Do you believe then...
...In taking off into flight
I hope and pray you will say
'Outta Sight'

I knew it when I saw your face
I don't know your name
It makes no difference just the same

Not a word ever spoken
There is no need
Words our spoken in silence with our eyes
...With our minds
You and I...A breed of a special kind

Oh, how I long to make you mine
With you my rainy days shine
You make them feel oh, so fine
Oh, How I love to cuddle beside you by firelight

I knew it when I saw your face
Now that I know your name
It makes a difference just the same

Peter LeBuhn

IN THE GROOVE OF THE NIGHT

In the Groove of the Night
Free of Fright
The Moon Shines Bright
Like a Spy

The tide Roars In
The exploration about to begin
I watch as this is Happenin'

In the Groove of the Night
The Portal of Passion found
Not Paying Attention to a sound

You Lost in Me
I in You

In The Groove of The Night
Our Passion Has Taken Flight

Peter LeBuhn

IN THE HUSH CALM OF THE TWILIGHT

In the hush calm of the twilight
When Day Becomes Night
No doubt Moonlight to trespass
On Our Eve
envisioning the glisten in your eyes
exposed to the moons angelical mood
As we lay laughing stylishly nude.

Performing Love Sonnets
The sheet music of our Hearts...Off The Charts
Delicate and Tender
intrigue of a love story surrounds the melody of our hearts
The flavor of stimulation, excitation, arousal
Wrapped in your arms

engrossing to my clutches
candles shine their flame blazing on our passions
The scent of sweet perfume
Drives my desire higher

The expression in your eyes
The sensation of your thighs
Succulent and sexy Before thee
endeavoring this pleasure
To savor the sweetness of you
In the exploration of you.

whispering poetry of passion
You lost in my body as time goes by
Lost in a erotic fashion
Thy body comes alive

Your the heat of my desire
My Passions...Into Action
Naked Before Each Other
As we Lay each other down
While you welcome my caress

your juicy sexy thighs
Makes me cry...With passion
Your flavor...I belabor
Your breasts like mountains
touching them loving them with a supple kiss

Lost inside your juices
To a sexy love experimentation
Passions Rise
Lost in all positions

Pleasure is the purpose
For
XTC is here
Wrapped inside my arms
Me Yours
To this explosive passion shared

No one can come asunder
This passion will take us higher
Only you can fill my heart
Beat my heart with desire

Peter LeBuhn

IN YOUR EYES

In Your Eyes
The Future Is Seen
In Your Eyes
The road is clear and clean
In Your Eyes
There is Happiness and Joy
In Your Heart
Much Love to Give
Ne'er to Depart
In Your Heart
The More You Give
The Greater Reward
In Your Hands
You take Mine
In Your Hands
You Take Mine

Peter LeBuhn

JUICY NECTER, WET LIPS

Gliding Thy fingers over your velvet soft hair
Admiring thy ripeness of your smooth blushed skin
Closer you come
The sweet parfame of you
In anticipation of how you must taste making my mouth water
Running my tongue along your groove and kiss you deeply
Sinking my lips gently onto your pink flesh
Juicy nectar wet my lips
Hunger for you all the more
Slow down...It is impossible
Delighting in your Love
Trying to catch your essence...All your juice as it goes quickly down
Taking of every last dropp to my mouth
My tongue deeper into your core
Eat you from the inside out
Greedily Drinking every droplet that flows from you
When you have poured all you are into me

Go in for more
For you were made to be savored
...To be loved...Like a Dove
Not simply devoured
My juicy peach

Peter B LeBuhn

JUNGLE LOVE

The time of year when Jasmine bloom,
most sweetly in the summer weather,
Helpless in the fragrant Jungle gloom,
On sultry night we spent together,
We, Love and Night, together blent,
A Trinity of trance content.

Your lips belong to me, wholly mine.
To kiss...To Drink....To Caress
Hearing from afar in faint distress
Sweet Wine One of Great Love Potions
To Set In Motion
The Fullness of Your Delight
With Our Passion
There Is No Fright
Taken In Abandon
Quivering note of Human Tremor
To rise and fall again,
In Shouts of ecstasy throughout the night,

Tasting the perfumed flower

In the moonlit hours

Tasting of the Jasmines flowers.

Peter LeBuhn

KISS OF A LOVER

To be kissed by my lovers mouth
Her Kiss is sweeter than wine.
To savor the ointments poured fourth in love.
Thy Name is as ointment poured forth,
An ointment to the heart.
How much I love thee.
Draw me Nearer
To will I follow
Your Chambers I rejoice in gladness
Fruitful are our vines
Remember we will Days Gone By
Days To Come
The keeper of my vineyards
Come drink with me,
Thy cheeks are rows of jewels,
Thy neck shines like gold.
Keep my vineyards with me
Behold, thou art fair

My love

A vision to behold,

With doves eyes

They do hypnotize.

This love Is One Love

To Be Lived in Much Love

Peter LeBuhn

LA BELLE DE LE TERRE

La Belle De Le Terre
Ma, Etre en amour
Ce'st un joile a la terrase
d'un cafe de amour

Je Parlez avec vous
Amour en mon couer
Venez Ici! ! !
Je Vous Appeler
Vous Regarder moi facon

Je fuir a elle
Tremper ma avec grande baisers
Peter LeBuhn

Peter LeBuhn

LAST DAYS

Last Days! ! !
Darkness rises over the moon
The wind swirling
Sand blowing over the plains
The landscapes at dusk are hues of orange and purple.

Tumbleweed is the only sight to be seen
What age is this?
Is this the End?
Are the wars about to begin?

The battle between The Four Horsemen
And the Angels from above
The earth is quiet.
The heavens are rumbling.
There is a battle plan in place.
To be one
To be righteous
To be Godly.

Peter LeBuhn

LAST OF THE GOLDEN BOYZ

My hey day
Time to make my noise

When you embark
Make your mark
...Shine...Shine
Show your spark

Let the World know
You are always going to
Hit a New Plateau

To have a flair
...To care
A clinician
With a mission

Last of the Golden Boyz

Shine...Shine You will receive your shrine

Peter LeBuhn

LE TIGRE PUISSANT

Le tigre puissant comme une perforation puissante puissante de faim de Thy de tigre par des yeux de mine car je projette mon mouvement sentant la chaleur sur le le dos de votre force de Thy de cou pendant que le tigre saisit votre corps donnant dans... lui dévore... goûtant votre chaque dernier morceau les augmentations de désir avec chaque goût de chair... Chaque baisse de sueur le tigre puissant une fois qu'il a goûté la viande l'apprivoise qu'il sera affamé d'elle toujours la lionne fera partie de lui son goût pour toujours dans lui aucun autre ne satisfera errer par implorer de la vie... Pour Son Un Amour

LIVE WIRE

Things going on Here and There
Things going on everywhere
Living in a world of craziness
Seems like life is a scare
Living on a live wire
Never sure when it is going to overload

Can't let it break me
Can't let is shake me
Got-ta beat the world at its' own game

Seems it's always been the same
Life is a crazy mixed up game
You have got to know who to listen to
You have got to play carefully
...Or you may end up
...Living on a Live Wire

Can't let it break me

Can't let is shake me

Got-ta take on the world

Got-ta beat the world at its' own game

Peter LeBuhn

LONELY IN THE NIGHT

Lonely in the Night
...I come to you
Unaware of my arrival
Around the corner
With a slight prowl
Seeing you peering
smiling out your joules

The intense moment here
For we know what will happen next
XXX
Yes
XXX
The Exploration of our bodies
Without fear
Diving in

Giving Pleasure...with no end in sight

To love you with all my might

Love to the Heights

Love to the Heights

Peter LeBuhn

LOVE

I just want to look into your eyes.
I want to feel your warm breath.
I want to see your smile and know that this smile is for me.
I want to be waken up by you rather than some kind of alarm clock.
I want to be your sunshine.
I want you to warm your hands up in the back pockets of my jeans.
I want you to pay me with your kisses for the rental of my jeans pockets.
I want to belong to you and. I am yours and you're mine.
I want to believe you and never question anything you say.
I want to hear your voice. I want to get to your inner thoughts.
I want to be everything you need. I want you to know all these things.
I want you to love me.
Can't wait for the moment I board the plane and start my final journey to you.

Peter LeBuhn

LOVE AT FIRST SIGHT

Feelings That I have No Control, No Power
As I stand before Thee In the Wild Flower.
Thy will is strong but overruled by Love and
Joyous Spirit.
Thy Emotions
Taken by Your Sweet Potion.
We are stripped, unclothed
Let the course of Love begin.
The Exploration...Impending
Where to start...Where to End
Two Flowers Budding
...Growing Together
The reason for this affaire
This ceremonial occasion
No man could Dare know

Behold Thee in Mine censured eyes
You My Love...To my surprise
Deliberate the love we make...and take
Who ever loved
There is love at first sight

Peter LeBuhn

LOVE IN MANY LANGUAGES

Hola
Bonjour
Ciao
Hallo
Las cosas del amor le traigo cosas del amor que le doy
Des choses de l'amour je vous apporte des choses de l'amour que je vous donne
Cose di amore porto voi le cose di amore che dò voi
Sachen der Liebe hole ich Ihnen Sachen der Liebe, die ich Ihnen gebe
Love in many languages
Love in many languages
The one language we all understand is love

Peter LeBuhn

LOVE,HOLY COW

Yes please call me
Answering to your call
My love
Thy being aroused once again
Passionately
A rhythm beats in your body
Hott in my pleasure package
Always hott
Having made love to you all last night
One more round
I need to hear the sound
The sound of your calling
When would you like the call?
You say
Call when ever the urge hits
The itch needs to be scratched

The chills you feel
Are real
You have once again aroused my being.
Passionately
beating a rhythm in my body! Holy cow!

Peter LeBuhn 2006

LOVES MAIDEN VOYAGE

Her love unbridled
She comes before thee
This midnight hour
Entering into my chambers
Unveiling what is hidden

As a ship on her maiden voyage
She charts her map on my body with care
More of a gift than St. Nicholas would leave there

Beginning from head
The soft supple kiss
The tender suck on the ear

The massage of the nipples on my pectoral
Slowly she sees land
Grabs for the anchor

With force
Pulling it
Up and Down

Shoving it in

Knowing here she will find treasure

The anchor she pulls

Finally she reaches

What she has cum for

Finally she has reached

What she has CUM for

Peter LeBuhn

LYRIC OF A LOVE SONG

The Lyric of a Love Song
Beats Softly on my heart
Unexpected Feelings
Could this be the healing

The hot sun beats down
Flowers all around
A connection...A friendship made
A year has passed since we saw
One another
Same time Next Year We say
Yet closer than ever
What we have will never sever

The way you look at me
As we sit and talk
in a Philadelphia Bar
Bruno's on Pine
This is an Amazing moment in time
Truly an Amazing moment in time

Peter LeBuhn

LYRICAL VERSES

Spilling lyrical verses
Keeping you warm
Your mind
Your thoughts
...Entranced
...At Every Glance
The lyrics I spill
bring thee closer
Feeling the warmth of your breast against mine
Whispering Secrets of Love in our ears
It appears
There is something here
You Lost in Me
I, You

They are the danger of Love
And the Pleasure of all things above

Peter LeBuhn

Maidens of the Sea (French)

Rememberence du beau vert ondule et les marées de mer jetant les demoiselles françaises libres avec les lèvres étouffantes… et les hanches ornent la beauté et le mystère des bateaux et la magie de la mer.

Peter LeBuhn

MIDNIGHT HOUR

The midnight hour
Thy moon high
Thy stars 'nigh
Willingly venturing into an unknown

Lights adorn the cobblestone streets
A little, little boy, plays feutball in yon churchyard past,

On all around their beauteous radiance cast,
This midnight hour.
All is quiet
Yet their is a riot
One that cannot be heard
Not a Word

Journeying o'er the path of life,
Onward, forward we move
With stars and northern lights o'er head in strife,
Perfect Bliss
Is This
The stars are out

For me
This midnight hour.

Rising High Does the full moon
Saying Hello to the Night
All of her shine and lustre

Bursting through the darkness wherein she was enshrined;
Arise, Arise
Willing, active, rapid thought
The past is the past as it intertwines the future
At midnight hour.

2006 Peter LeBuhn

MIDNIGHT JUICES

The sensations As you come upon thee
How you pressed down upon me
My body yields to your curves and contours
your eyes spoke sexual hunger
your hunger for me.
My body for I offered
as your canvas
My mouth was dry in remembrance
of the taste of your sweet juicy love
The Heat, The beat
the smoothness of its slide;
and I became drunk on the
scent of your ardor,
ready to be taken.

I declare myself your mystery To find the answers in your passion.
Is it me that you long for.
Let me ignite your fires of lust
To places that have never been awakened before
the moon sleeps her last breaths
Suddenly she awakens to our sounds and screams of love.

My body rises
packed away a gift for you to lay
between solstice and equinox,
my body rises up of the mattress
Three feet we go
these eyes did not raise.
Your thighs are wild, whet, filled with juice
horses, awaiting your
ride.

And our flesh on flesh
ignited in a blazing fire,
The likes of which No man can match desire
We fucked on
Cashmere,
made love on Egyptian Cotton
On Age old hieroglyphics
The Pharos did write.

diamonds Adorn your eyes
images of you on the sheets

I awaken to the

Wet of your tongue

Licking my

Midnight Juices

Peter LeBuhn

MIGHTY TIGER

Like a powerful mighty tiger
Thy hunger piercing through mine eyes
As I am planning my move
Feeling the heat on the back of your neck
Thy Strength as The tiger grips your body
Giving in...He is devouring...Tasting
Your every last morsel
The desire increases with each taste of flesh...
Every dropp of sweat
The mighty tiger once he has tasted the meat
Tames Him
He will hunger for Her always
The Lioness will be part of him
Her taste forever in him
No other will satisfy
Wandering through Life
Craving...
For His One Love

Peter LeBuhn

MOLTEN LOVE

Lowering your thighs
...To mine
Set to take your ride
Lay me down on my bed
...rolling into the shadows
of the night
Entering into a never world
...without a care...we dare
There is no fright
With Passion...Carnal Lust
Tasting you, Like a thirst,
AWAKENING
The fires within you
Ride, Ride
Release The Lava
Of the passion feast,
Ride, Ride

My thickness deep down to my soul,
Ride, Ride Till I die of desire,
Release the Molten Lava,
Molten
And Gold.

Peter LeBuhn

MONDAY FLOWERS

Like Monday flowers, you sew your thoughts of love at my feet to propose to me.

Your bond, ours, a resemblance of me and you. Together for a lifetime, longer to be true.

My heart beckons to you, crying to be held, and with yours it does so melt.

One-we are a blending...body, soul, mind.

In ecstasy we writhe, rising on tidal waves of lust. As our bodies inner cores, burst showering one another in our pure, silken love.

My body is yours. Your temple, your concubine of pure sex, an unadulterated bond.

Your fingers strumming humming over me making the throbbing spread without.

My skin, yours, damp, slick with our love.

Your fingertips dancing in our sweet nectar, for us to taste the flavor of Monday flowers.

Peter LeBuhn 2010

MUSIC HALL FUNK

The moon has risen
Venturing down a dark back alley
The night is misty

In the far off distance
Hearing music
....people playing
....people singing
....people dancing

It is a music hall
down a cobblestone street
Slipping in the side door
The music overtakes me
....into a fierce dancing beat

Noticing two ladies by the bar
checking me
Playing to them and dance increasingly seductively

They are coming upon me
The dream has begun
The fantasy...Set in Place
....The dance we will make
....The future is ours is to see
....The future is ours to take

Peter LeBuhn

MY ANGEL

Coming into my life
On a breeze
One cool September eve
You found the door of my heart
and began to play
Beautiful music...I heard
at the start
Lightly I could hear the pitter pat of the drums
as you would talk with me
Then as the conversation continues
In comes the string quartet
Beautiful Music
My Angel
Seeing you from across the room
For you now I swoon
I live for you
I love for you
You are my reason
You are my Angel

MY CHINA ROSE

The cold wind blows
In the white of the snow
catching a glimpse of you
walking like a china rose

I testify
To the heights of the sky
You I cannot let fly by

This china rose
The way she looks at me
With a certain prose
My heart glows

Her smile
Has made it all worthwhile
My China Rose

Peter LeBuhn

MY FIRST LOVE

I met you at Cafe de Margots
A beautiful sunny morning in Paris
Me...The American man in a foreign land
You...The belle of the land.
We talked and spoke of life and love
You took my hand and made your stand.
'Meet me at L'Hotel D'Paris' you said
Fearful I paused but my heart said yes.
I agree.
The hour approaches
I am wearing the colors of your country
Blue jacket, white pants, red striped shirt.
WOW! My heart beats as I see you
wearing your turquoise taffeta sundress.
We are to dine at L'Tour de Eiffel
I am living a dream
I offer to pay...She insists she must
for she asked me. We venture down the
streets of Paris We embrace in a waterfall.
You taught me the meaning of Love.
Walking Hand in Hand...Arm In Arm

Approaching The Hotel Of Paris
Dripping Whet
Ascending to the room
Undressing and Drying each other off passionately…simultaneously
You wear my white cotton dress shirt and a beautiful pink thong
Putting the Beautiful French Music On.
Sabrina…You Dance Around Me
Take Me in Your Arms
This Man in a Foreign Land…Fallen Prey to your charms.
We Make Love all night inside each others silken bodies.
The morning comes early
Things to do…Studies ahead
Understanding that this may come to an end
'Sabrina I understand if you are not here when I return'
Responding quickly 'No, No I will be here I want to be with you'
Sabrina, Thank you…For You Have taught me what Love Is
You Have Taught Me What Love Is.
Peter B LeBuhn

MY LATINA ROSE (SPANISH)

Los soplos fríos del viento en el blanco de la nieve que cogía una ojeada de usted que caminaba como una Latina se levantaron Le atestiguo a las alturas del cielo que no puedo dejar la mosca cerca Esta Latina se levantó la manera que ella me mira con cierta prosa brilla intensamente mi corazón Su sonrisa le ha hecho todo el de mérito mi Latina rose

Peter LeBuhn

MY POTION

The sun radiates her beams upon the sand
This world, truly grand
The quietness of the ocean
The tide in forward motion
It is my potion.

Vizions of Dolphin
Swimming 'fore me
Nothing compares
To this feeling from within.

Alone in the vast creation
As life was meant to be
This spiritual sensation
The sights, smells and sounds

By the hands of what stylist could have painted this picture?
What Genius?
What Virtuoso?

Giving Thanks for this creation
with feeling of elation.

Humbled, feeling modest
In a world so large and powerful.
Grateful for this Gift To enjoy.

Peter LeBuhn

NATURE IN ALL HER FLAVOR

Nature
(In all her flavor)
Silently speaks
through her radiant beauty

She greets each day with a sense of duty
Rising over the horizon
The sun slowly awakes
O'er the unfettered waters
Singing in Each day with new Psalters.
Nature
(In all her flavor)
Silently speaks
through her radiant beauty
The Landscape Framed by
Green Pine and Fur Trees
Sights and Sounds of the seagulls
In their home.
The banging of the water on the shores
Sights of the sea white water
as it fiercely rolls in.

Nature

(In all her flavor)

Silently speaks

through her radiant beauty

The white sands

through my toes

The wind in my hair

The fresh sea air

Nature

(In all her flavor)

Silently speaks

through her radiant beauty

Peter LeBuhn

OH WHAT A WORLD!!!

Oh What A World
She takes me for a twirl
Accidental encounters
Crystal counters
Oh What A World
Every significant moment
Vital...In the blink of an eye
Life Changing...With Nature's Wind
Every Decision made.
Oh What A World
Life takes us for a twirl
Life-Saving, Life -Altering
Appreciation for what is given.
Bestowed upon thy world my love.
It is A gift from above
Oh What A World
Continents collide

So Far in Destination

Yet so close in ideology

So Close Yet So Far

So Far Yet So Close

Peter LeBuhn

Ojos Españoles

En su sorpresa agradable de los ojos
A usted roba mi corazón usted que no saldré
Mis sistemas son van mientras que emprendemos
nuestra misión del amor
En sus brazos caliente y cierre su latido del corazón
contra el mío que usted es thine
En mi mente usted está allí toda la hora
Mi vida mi amor mi lealtad para usted

Peter

OLDE GLORIES...NEW PROMISES

The Glories of the Olde
The Promise of Things Yet to come
What will guide thee
What roads will be taken.

Thankful for what little has been
Keeping thy cup watered.
For what was once small
Will grow in abundance

The Glories of the Olde
The Promise of Things Yet to come
Never to Forget
The beginning...The promise made to my country
...My God...My World
To fulfill these Glories
Into Greater Promise

OUR HEARTS UNCHARTED

You smile to Me From afar
Your name It is unknown
My heart warms to roaring flame.
The drum beats become louder by the
Second.

Still, you do not speak
Yet you are inviting me into
your world.
A WORLD of the Unknown
Many Pages will be written
On blank sheets from our hearts.

The course of this story is
uncharted. No one else has
read our book. Not even us.

I will find out who you are

and as for the pages. The first

Entry will be You.

Peter LeBuhn

Paris I adorent

France, her mystery
Her history
Around each corner
A story unfolds

The quietness of La Seine
The elaborateness of Le Tour Eiffel
Paris I adorent
As it is you I explore
We have developed rapport

En Paris ces't ma couer
En Paris ces't ma maison

One day we will meet again
One day we will meet again

Peter LeBuhn

Paris It is My Home (French)

La lucarne de Paris brille sur votre pièce rose en matin tôt. Portraits des portraits de mer scènes de canotage de Monet et de Renoir... de serene Vous saunter à votre miroir intégral vous vous peignez les cheveux soyeux mous. La joie est à votre coeur... que vous avez trouvé le paradis. Votre promenade de matin vous commence passage que le sourire de de jardin A de fleur de Luxemborg Gardens Le Belle scintille outre de votre visage l'arc De Trimphe... le symbole des libertés De France La beauté continue les champions Elysees et la Concorde À Paris vous avez trouvé votre coeur votre amour votre maison

Peter LeBuhn

PASSION INTO ACTION

The Moon Shines Bright
You Hold Thee Tight
Secure In Your Arms
Taken by your Charms
Lost in Passions
That I will not Ration
The Cold Wind Blows
Through Our Bodies
My Body On Fire
To You I Aspire...To Desire
To Take Thee Higher
A flame has been lit
illuminated, ablaze
With Passion
Taken into action
Take Me
Explore Me
Become One With Me

Peter LeBuhn

PEACE
A poem written in 75 minutes on a trip to Baltimore, MD.

Speak to me of serenity, of treasures yet to be found, of peace that flows
like a river. Tell me of tranquil places that no hand has marred, no storm
has scarred. Give me visions of standing in sunlight or the feeling of
spring mist against my cheek as I live and move and breathe.
Show me paths that wind through the wild lilies and beds of buttercups.
Sing me songs like the mingled voices of wrens and meadowlarks, the
lowing of gentle cows, the soft mother-call of a mare to her colt.
Lead me past a glass-smooth pond where frogs croak of coming-out
parties, their graduation from frisky tadpoles to squat green frogs.
Find me a place in the sunlight to sit and
think and listen to the sweet inner voice that says so quietly, 'Peace, be still.'

Peter LeBuhn 2008

PEACE IN A HECTIC WORLD

The Cold Wind Blows
It speaks loudly as I venture along.
The autumn leaves are falling.
A reminder that Winter
Soon will be here
I try to keep my heart warm
though reminders of death
all around me
The leaves have fallen
The cold has set in.
But Wait! ! !
There is beauty all around me
All of creation
a gift from thee
The deer and the animals they run about.
The streams and the rivers running.

Almost speaking silently...peacefully
Truly in this hectic world
There is peace
There is peace

Peter LeBuhn

PENETRATING LOVE

Unforgettable this instant,
Mazed in your eyes.
The beginning of a climax
The flood tides of thy passion
Break the levy of thy heart
You ne'er to depart

indulging to treasure your sweetness.,
stimulating tongues tangle.
Thy heart aches
Wait No Longer Can I for you to take

On thy back
Pleading with thy heart
Those lips come calling
For they have heard

Rising up High
On My thigh
Greeted with a Passion Stare
The Language of Love
You Are Aware

Reservation for two
you enter with no hesitation,
Sitting Firm
Riding with pleasure

Taunt me, tease me,
grin on your face,
You have put me in place

Then suddenly
Hair Flying
You Riding...Wildly
Granting Relief.

Happiness comes upon you
knowing I now have peace.

Taking and Penetrating thy pride,
Charging and thrusting You were deep inside.

Feet upon chest

Your sweet nectar
It is the best

Scream loud like never before
Cross the rooftops
Down The alleyways.
When places reached cut to the core.
Must Have More
Must Have More

Slowing, then come 'please-don't-stop' pleas,
Whimpering I'm at your mercy.

in our entrancing dance,
Our eyes fixed in a glance
Curious expressions
Bodies in full view

'Tween thy thighs
as you deeper dive
My power made alive

'Don't think of leaving'
MMMMMMMMMMMH
All of this heavy breathing

'Don't Leave
We are About to Hit X-T-C'
Navigating my body
You climb high
You are the captain
Ready to ride

To the Edge of Nowhere
That is where to go
To the Edge of Nowhere...and everywhere

Gauging perfect rhythm between us two.
Panting hard, with quivering shakes,
Not much more can either take,
As each resists the pulsing throbs,
Not wanting to be one who robs.
But there's no stopping from this flight,
Wildly heading for realms beyond night,
Each to our own promised lands we go,
Worlds imagined, the other never knows.
And upon return to this earthly place,
The visit lasting just seconds in space,
We find each other coming back to ground,
From a paradise we each together found!
Peter LeBuhn

Peter LeBuhn: A Biography

Some say He is A simple man
Some Say Complex
Some say Full of Passion
Some Say Spirit Filled

A Gift Has Been Given
For Thee to Share with the
World
My Life
My Love
My Heart

Peter LeBuhn is all of these
His words speak volumes
Touch hearts
As he cares for others humbly

His Life is Not His Own

For He Is A Gift To The World

He only aims to please one Master

Jesus Christ

Peter LeBuhn

PLEASURES OF THY HEART

My Love Come to be with thee
The pleasures of our hearts will prove
Valleys Green
Rolling in the Groves and Fields

By Shallow Waterfalls
I sing to thee my Songs
Doves circle above in approval
As your golden locks unfurl
In the rose petals 'neath us

Your eyes pull thine closer
Closer to you...Not a word
Yet you speak loudly with your heart

These pleasures of our hearts
Ne'er to part
These pleasures of our hearts
Struck by the Loving Dart.

Peter LeBuhn

Première Passion(French)

Consacré à Sabrina, la belle de Paris qui m'a enseigné ce qu'est l'amour Je vous ai rencontré au beau matin ensoleillé de Cafe de Margots A à Paris je... l'homme américain dans une terre étrangère vous... la belle de la terre. Nous takled et rai de la vie et vous aimons avons pris ma main et avons fait votre stand. 'rencontrez-moi à vous de L'Hotel D'Paris que ledit craintif j'a fait une pause mais mon coeur a indiqué oui. Je conviens. Les approches d'heure je porte les couleurs de votre veste bleue de pays, pantalon blanc, chemise rayée rouge. DÉFAUT DE LA REPRODUCTION SONORE! Mes battements de coeur comme je vous vois porter vos sundress de taffetas de turqoise. Nous devons diner chez L'Tour de Eiffel I vis un rêve que j'offre au salaire... elle exige qu'elle doit pour elle m'a demandée. Nous osons en bas des rues de Paris que nous embrassons dans une chute deau. Vous m'avez enseigné la signification de l'amour. La marche de concert... bras dans le bras approchant l'hôtel de l'égoutture de Paris whet monter à la salle déshabillant et se séchant outre passionément... simultanément de vous usage ma chemise de robe blanche de coton et une belle lanière rose mettant la belle musique française dessus. Sabrina... que vous dansez autour de moi me portez dans des vos bras cet homme dans une proie tombée étrangère de terre... à vos charmes. Nous faisons à amour toute la nuit à l'intérieur de chaque autres les corps de soie. Le matin vient des choses tôt pour

faire… l'Arrangement d'études en avant que ceci peut se terminer
'Sabrina que je comprends si vous n'êtes pas ici quand je renvoie
'répondre rapidement 'non, aucun je serez ici je voulez être avec vous
'Sabrina, merci de vous m'ont enseigné que quel amour est vous m'avez
enseigné ce qu'est l'amour.

Peter B LeBuhn

PUERTO RICO

You are in my stocking hung with care
Sights of Puerto Rico... Outside are there
Whooooooooooooosing Waves
The sea breeze
Just you and me
All that matters... you and me
Diamonds in your eyes
I have made you mine
Traveling through the ruins of the city
The churches... the castles
The Museums... Paintings of El Greco Adorn
Living a dream
near an island stream
Hypnotized by your eyes
Your touch
Your love
Your tenderness

Peter LeBuhn

RHYTHM OF THE NIGHT

Seduced by the rhythms of the night
Sounds of People Laughing
People Singing
People Dancing
Entices me nearer to the source
The night streets covered in fog
I venture down the cobblestone streets
to find the source
The sounds of the street beat
that move my feet
The music emanates from a dark alley
through a side door.
The music Pumping...Thumping
set afire by the music
The music and my soul become one
My feet dance aflutter
Shutter I think to what the future holds

As you and I embrace into one body

Engulfed into One

Nothing around us matters

Just You and I

Peter B LeBuhn

SEXUAL FIRE FROM WITHIN

There is a fire within us..
that only needs a touch to bring forth flame.
Passion ignites...
when I hear you whisper my name.
My body shivers... oh...
but not from cold...
but from the sweet anticipation...
of a desire that never seems to grow old.
I lay my head upon your chest..
kiss your skin softly.
breathing the manly scent of me...
Intoxicating you like fine wine...
making your senses whirl...
Your hands...
are softly caressing my back...
making me melt...
yet every nerve is tingling...
with the need of you.
You gently lift me up and softly kiss my forehead
Sending chills all down my spine
Can't wait the anticipation...

Softly kiss up your body gently caress our lips...
My body fills with excitement and anticipation
Hands roaming each others bodies
Filling the silkiness of your skin
My heart starts pounding from pleasure
As your fingers run over my treasures
Gently sliding the key in as you begin to turn
Gently stroking my body
OHHHH MY GOD is all I could whisper...
Our passion increases...
Our souls ignited...
You lower down and kiss me passionately
and I know I am in Heaven
For I saw the flames burning in your eyes.

SILENCE

Silence Golden
In this moment
Though the silence

Many thoughts are spoken
Something happening
A strange occurrence
that cannot be unbroken

Your smile stretches a mile
Bright as the sun
Blinding...Yet I go nearer
Thy heart becomes undone
It becomes clearer

You are the One
You are the One

Peter LeBuhn

SILENTLY NAKED

Silent
The gentle voice of the waterfalls
Only to keep us company
Knee-deep drenched in water
Through the darkness
As it becomes light
Through a flicker of soft-blue
Off the rocks surface

NAKED
You are waiting for me
In the warm deep water
Your arms stretched along the pool side
Under the falls

Momentarily standing on the opposite edge
Giving you a glance of me
All to Enjoy
Turning sideways and poise in silhouette
Letting my naked outline work its spell on you.

Slowly making my move to my prey
Gliding towards you
A water-snake seeking its mesmerized prey

You wait
Unmoving
As I reach you
I can see the smile on your face
You know that you are being seduced
And love every moment

I hold my face upturned to you
My lips open in silent temptation
You bend to me
Our lips meet
Our tongues flicker together

Desire communicated

Reaching down
You feeling my hardness
Waiting....Waiting
for Climax

No more preliminaries
No more foreplay

Wrapping your legs around mine
lowering yourself onto me

The gentle motion of our bodies
Creates tiny waves
Rippling rhythmically against the pool side

Peter LeBuhn

SING A NEW SONG

Singing to each new day a new song
Sing out Strong
Thy Life, it is thy song
Thy song is thy gift

The gift to be given to everyone
All across the earth
A song for all nations
Tribes, tongues

Songs of honor and majesty
will be sung
Joyous sounds from many lungs
Man, Woman, Child

Rejoice, Again Rejoice
'Let the Heavens be glad and the earth rejoice;
Let the sea roar, and all that fills it' (Psalm 96: 11)

The skies will open up
The brightness will blind us
This is the day we meet our Lord
Our Creator
Our Savior

Peter LeBuhn

SLICE OF TIME

Sailing Through Life
On A Breeze
Entering in
A Beautiful woman
Stealing part of my life
Taking this slice
Making it hers
With her pirate smile

heart being stolen
thoughts on the girl
Unsure what will unfurl
That Slice of time
You own from me

Slice of time
Precious
In the right place at the right time
The right woman
The right man....

On A Breeze

On A Slice

A single second

Changes our whole life

Peter LeBuhn

SLOW SEX

With my tongue
Exploring
Attempting to memorize her reactions
Thy fingers followed the avid contour
exploiting her body's gentle persuasions

Thy loving, sexual words pleased her senses
extending the nine to ten
Boldness dismounted the neutral fence
Creative imagination became a randy mix

Five minutes slowly marched to forty-five
Each second seemed a lifetime
The sex was morally alive
Sensations just about blew my mind

We're into the late morning
after a limping pause
The benefits were truly rewarding
We will revisit the act because...

The very short night quickly slipped
into eternities book of history
The lessons left me fully equipped
to find the elusive g-spot instinctively

SO HOT, SO PASSIONATE

I want to touch the warmth of your body,

And feel the heat of your skin.

I want to be the only one

That satisfies you...

The one to wet the sheets on your bed,

I want you,

To feel my seduction and my passion

To leave the prints of my burning fire

Within your soul...

SOLVING FOR THE UNKNOWN

In Search of the answer
Solving for the Unknown
Many Questions
...Lead to Many Answers
...Many Answers
...Lead to Many Questions
Never stop the search
We should always be on the perch
Solving for the Unknown
For what was not known
Is now of knowledge
A new page written in history
And a new page to be turned

Peter LeBuhn

SPANISH EYES

In your eyes
A pleasant surprise
You steal my heart
You I will not depart

My Systems Are Go
As we embark on our mission of love

In your arms
Warm and close
Your Heartbeat against mine
You are thine

In my mind
You are there
All the time

My life

My love

My loyalty

For you

Peter LeBuhn

Storybook Memories of Puerto Rico(Spanish)

Usted está en mi media colgada con vistas del cuidado de Puerto Rico... Fuera de hay las ondas de Whoooooooooooosing la brisa del mar apenas usted y yo todo que importe... usted y yo los diamantes en sus ojos que le he hecho la mina que viajaba con las ruinas de la ciudad los churchs... los castillos los museos... Las pinturas del EL Greco adornan vivir un cercano ideal una corriente de la isla hipnotizada por sus ojos su tacto su amor su dulzura

Peter LeBuhn

THE BEAVER

She was a sexy beaver went on a journey that leading her here
all the way here to from the Pacific.
Parking herself between my legs
taking me deeper
Quickly undressing
My beaver was in for the loving of a lifetime.
Her licking so sweet on my massive member
taking it all the way down her throat
she is my sweet fortune cookie.
She was now ready for the loving of a lifetime!

Peter LeBuhn

THE CALL

Would you like to have sex before pleasure
Take me now...I am burning with desire
Get Down on Me honey
Too much of a good thing is wonderful
I am bringing in home darling
Now...Attached to You...As One
You taking thee deep
You smile
It is the second best thing that you do with your lips.
Sit...Sit on me Gently
Take me in
Take me deep
Kiss me...Hold me...Guide me into you
The rain will fall
I will rain on you
Cumming whenever you call
You have heard my mating call
Answered you have

Into your arms

Your sexual charms

I am lost

I am lost

THE DANCE

In the hills of green
And the Sunshine's sheen
Like a panther...your beauty
and grace came about thee
without a warning...without a
trace.
Entranced by your charms
You are like royalty
Humble wearing your arms.
Words are not spoken
It is understood
The dance has begun
The future is love

Peter B LeBuhn

THE EXOTIC ETERNAL DANCE

Marvelous and graceful, Plentiful breasts
Beautiful posterior Shaved soft and silky
She is beautiful Stargazing her belly dance
Sensuous movements of the hips
Watching her body Maneuvering to the melody
Arching her back Tossing her hair
She is dancing, prancing for me
Kissing me with her eyes
As I kiss her with mine
She is nearly through
Following her to the back
Waiting for her to follow
It does not take long
I grabbed a handful of her hair...with passion
Pulling her bosom to mine French kissing her
Soft and gentle at first
Then not so soft
Sliding my tongue down her body
Taking my time at her nipples
On her belly, on her clit
Plunging my tongue into her treasure

She tasted sweet and tart all at once

Sliding my fingers into her tight body

She tensed as I caressed her g-spot

Nursing on her clit...Feeling her body rock

Seeing her eyes roll in passion....in pleasure

Hearing her cries of X-T-C

Her body spasmodic

Silken ribbons of her nectar ran down my chin

Climbing her body kissing her deeply

Letting her taste herself on my tongue

She would dance for me again

The Dance Eternal

The Expressionless Page

To an expressionless page
My pen takes action
The words of my heart flow
with passion.
A story is being written
A drama
A comedy
A tragedy (I hope not)
For in my heart
I know what is real
and true.
Every moment...Every second
The pen is making a new entry
The page now has meaning
and feeling
History is being made.
Where will my pen take me
The future will be seen.

Peter B LeBuhn

THY FAITHFUL SERVANT

Thy Beloved
Invisible thy to you
You to I
Yet Bound by our Fathers love on High
All of these bodies.
Make Up One Nation Under God
There is no true life without the Father
The Son
The Holy Spirit
His Spicket
Drenches us in his Love
He Loves Every One
Why Then, Do You Search for answers?
The answer is clear
Christ is saying to you
I AM HERE! ! !
The quest within you
from whence born again
The transformation was to begin
Walking in Blind Faith
Though Seeing More Clearly

The Lord Is By Our Side

He is Our General

To Lead us in our battles

We strive for Perfection

Falling short of His Grace Each Time

Knowing We are Human

Accepts Us Lovingly

He Stretches out his hands with the mighty key of Love

Faith ,Hope, Love

The Greatest of these is Love He said

This is How my Father in Heaven Lived

So Shall I

By opening the door, you shall wake the Father.

Well Done Good and Faithful Servant! ! ! !

Well Done! ! !

Peter LeBuhn

THE FEAST

Making you a feast
A feast to remember
The table adorned with fixins
You come to the table waiting
Waiting to be served
Out of nowhere
Coming to your table
Naked...Bare...RAW
Thy COCK only inches from your face
As your meal is being dished
Serving you your drink
Taking in a sweet sausage
A few bites you have to be nourished
Hardly touching your food
Otherwise your mind occupied
You attack me
In lust

What was going to happen just happened
We discover our carnal love for each other
The discovery
The taste of each other
Like Strawberry Wine
You taste fine
Like Strawberry Wine

THE FORBIDDEN KISS

The sweet aroma, fragrance of Thy indulgent fantasies
Your shadow, sexy silhouette approaches
...In the midnight hour
Frightened yet excited.... drawing closer
closer you take me into your body and soul
Longing for the kiss..
The forbidden Kiss
The forbidden fruit... that only your kiss does hold
Gazing at each others cherry lips with total astonishment
As if hypnotized...Drawing nearer...Closer
Longing for them to meet mine
Seeking to drink them in like a fine wine
This kiss...This Forbidden Kiss...So Sweet...Never Ending
Tasting the taste of raspberry wine
so splendid... on your lips

Interlocked in each others Arms...Legs

Forever Will This wonderful kiss

Be sought

Knowing, Hoping

Forever will be Forbidden

Peter LeBuhn

THE GIFT OF LIFE

The Gift of Life
Ours to treasure
In all its splendor
The gift given from above
With Free Love
The Responsibility of the Gift Lay
With Us
To Confess
His Success
The Gift of Life
When I wake up
I taste of the Lords' Loving Cup
'This is the day the Lord Hath Made'
'Rejoice' 'Rejoice' and be Glad in it
For this life He has carefully knit
Everything that happens seems to fit
The Gift Of Life
I owe to My God...My Father
My Lord in Heaven

Peter LeBuhn

HEIGHTS OF LOVE

The Heights of Love
Gentle Stroking
Sensuous cloaking
Coming before thee Bare, Open and Raw.
Your Gentle Hands
Slide across and down my body
In tender motion.
By The second...Going Faster
Like A Steam Locomotion.
Gripped By Your Soft Supple Hands
Taking Me Deep...Into Your Throat
Thick Into your Body

Throbbing rhythmically, Pulsating Stronghold
Over My Shaft.
Truly this is a pleasure craft.
Generous with your fellatio
Thy stimulation takes thee higher
My heart accelerating, flying in delicious Passion
Ejaculate over your sensual palate and tongue
You express your pleasure

as we enter a Passion Of No Return.

The feeling mystifying, gratifying.

You tasting my Love Potion

With all your Emotion.

...Hmmmm

...Ohhhh

I thirst, crave, desire for you further

As Our affaire endures.

You have brought me to the Heights of Love

You have brought me to the Heights of Love

Peter LeBuhn

THE INVINCEABLE TIGER

Unlimited Power
The Tiger watches over us
Ultimate Protection and Care.
Evil not to enter
Not even to Dare.
The Mighty Tiger
Ever Watching
Ever Knowing
...Her Family
Keeping the dynasty intact
So Strong their possession attract.
Kingly...Queenly
With Sovereign Grace.
Over Their Place.
The Mighty Tiger
Invincible
The Mighty Tiger
Forever Shall Reign

Peter LeBuhn

THE JOURNEY

Beleaguered and Beaten
Burned to a crisp
My faith I have lost
What is to become of this?
The Fire burns brightly...The ashes spread widely.
All I feel is death
Lord how do I get out of this?
The light flickers only dim
But flicker it does
For The answer now is known
I have lost everything only to regain it
Trials and toils
They do boil in the deep of my soul
My burning and yearning to do right
With all thy might
I humble thyself in thy sight
The journey has been long...now I am strong

Peter LeBuhn

THE KEY TO YOUR HEART

Let me find the key to your heart so I can unlock your secret chambers of love when I do find that key, I will lock myself in your heart forever..

THE KISS

Your lips featheriness sensation of your lips
as they slide over mine
Taste like honey to my soul
Taking me to a different place in time

You please at the hot fire of my torch
As I pleasure your tender silken breasts
Thy passion craved
Released by the nectar of your kiss-sss

The drumming of my heart beats in rhythm with yours
Slowly...Then more rapidly
Your skin
A river of light
My moan
Pleasures you as you start
Ecstasy I'd never fight

A lovers tune dances up my spine
As the shadow of your embrace
slides across my thighs

ohhh sooo slowly the pace

Our hearts mingled in rapture
The torture of passion so sweet
The affection of a thousand years
As at least we meet

The motion of our rhythm
in perfect unison we move
our flight those of doves
As we reach heavens hymen

Peter LeBuhn

THE LIVING SONG

Sing a new song everyday
Live your song
For the song comes from deep within
You are the song
Sing it
Sing it
Loud like Thunder
The seas will part
The heavens will open
In pleasing
Sing a New song
Sing a New song

Peter LeBuhn

THE MAGIC OF LOVE IN THE MOONLIGHT

Seeing you from a distance,
Dressed in cool white
The sweet curves of your body shine through
At long last our meeting
Our eyes
How they glisten
Outlined against the shimmering sands.
Getting closer to each other
The Stars how they shine into a myriad
of twinkling lights celebrating in harmony with joy as
they felt love wafting between us.

Very close to you
No room between us
Seeing a smile from those ruby lips, inviting a kiss.
Taking you in my arms and gaze deeply in your eyes.
The look of love, Desire
Wanting
Needing
The warmth of your body
Against the beat of thy heart.

Kissing gently at first,
Lips brushing each others.
A tap dance into passion
Knowing we cannot resist.
Your lips part
Our tongues dance together,
kissing deeper and with passion.
My heart bats faster.
Our senses command
Our bodies Demand
As we lie on the white sands,
the waves lapping at our feet, I ask, 'Shall we swim my darling? '
'Shall we swim in Love'

THE ONES THAT GOT AWAY…THE ONE THAT STAYED!!!

Lived a life of Lost Loves
Scars across my body
From each woman who has poisoned me
Still…My love for the fairer sex remains.

All of you got away
In Search of Love I say?
Wait a minute! …Someone new?
Peering across a smoke filled room
The Glimpse of you in the alley

You stop…You look at me with your
Beautiful Brown Eyes
The message is clear
In your hesitation
You are the one that will stay

Peter LeBuhn

THE OPEN DOOR

The open door
Many times clouded by our
blind sight...We cannot see
This door never closes for it
is our way of future opportunity
The rain may fall
Our life may stall
The door is our vision to go on
Walk through the door
Questions will be answered
Your life will become clear
What is my purpose for being here?

Peter B LeBuhn

THE QUITENESS OF MY HEART

I see you in the quietness of my heart
Your presence is felt with every beat
Your smile...Your radiance
shines from across the room blinding me
in a frenzy of warm happiness.
This day we are to spend together
In the midst of our hearts
Our minds...Our thoughts
In one accord.
Happiness has entered me at last
At last I am happy

Peter LeBuhn

THE SPIRIT WITHIN

The Spirit in me meets the same Spirit in you
saluting the divine in you
saluting the Light of God in you.
bringing together my body and soul,
focusing my divine potential,
bowing to the same potential within you.
bowing to the divine in you.
recognizing that within each of us is
a place where Divinity dwells,
when we are in that place, we are One.

Peter LeBuhn

THE TAPESTRY OF WHO WE ARE

Thy conscious journeys wistfully,
Into The Past,
Responding Passionately to the present
Through this journey
The mystique of you
Erotically defined and redefined
On second thoughts is just evanescent.
Reveal your silhouette
Coming unto Thee
Presenting yourself over Bent Pillow
Enjoying My device
Delighting in the vigor
High on the bed canvas, your soft belly cushioned,
Your fingers tremble knowing not what to do with themselves
Forgotten dissuasion? Then wait for the motion -
Tight rhythmic stroking, an insistent delve
Of snaking tongues as you are taken,
Again and again in your riotous mind,
Forever, beliefs can be shaken
Love Taken
Since cosseting verse hardly serves to remind.

Now is the instant to crawl on those knees,
You make your plea
Bent over pillows,
You'll steal the show,
Love of magnificent tapestry
Nothing will soften the blow.
To Find a New Truth
Sharing complicity,
The threads that weave 'tween us
This is the tapestry of who we are
The tapestry of who we are

Peter LeBuhn

THE TEACHER

Are you the Teacher?
...The question is asked
...Yes...Yes is the Response
A cold wind blows
A bus suddenly pulls forward
What is about to happen
...Life changing
Off the Bus
Approaches the Son
The Teacher, The Father Responds
Arms open wide
My son! My son!
You have come home
Where you belong
Next to the Fathers Side

Peter LeBuhn

THE VESSEL

Put on earth as a Vessel
To be used for His will
Every move that is made
will determine the future
How our time will be filled

The Word to be preached
In the way we live our lives
Our Talents we nurture
Help them to grow

Without the Utterance of your Name
People see you in your people
Through our works you will see our
Faith and Our Love For God Above
The talents we have our gifts from God
How we use them our gift to him

Peter B LeBuhn

THE TIGRESS (LONELY IN THE NIGHT)

The Tigress
Lonely in the Night
Her Mate Away For a Journey
Longs for His Return
Dreaming
Thoughts of the touch
She loves so much
The smooth caress against her body
The 'Purring' against her neck
The passion and love
Between the two
Cannot be matched
No other above
The tiger will come home
From far off
Slowly approaching
...The Tigress

....Her head lifts...she knows his scent

They are together again at long last

At long last

There will be love

Once Again

Peter LeBuhn

Theatre De Amour

Qu' est -ce que tu fais cet apris-midi, Mon Cheri
Il y a un cinema dans ma quartier de mon couer
On y va?
On y va?

Ne Partez pas! ! !
Venez Ici! ! !

D'abord, nous allons
au theatre de amour

Je desirer vous
Je desirer vous

Peter LeBuhn

Peter LeBuhn

THEATRE OF THE UNKNOWN

I saw you out of the corner
of my eye
gnashing your teeth
Looking almost half way shy
I know I saw you before
I can't place it where
Maybe in that bar
Or was it that night under the stars
Are you following me
Should I speak
You peer at me
You make not a peep
Only can I imagine your thoughts
when the smoke is cleared
You disappear
Once Again
This has been a
Theatre of the Unknown! ! !

Peter B LeBuhn

THESE DREAMS

These dreams of these, So genuine, So true

You and I, delight, in a horse and carriage
ride on a winter day in the city, as we ride.
Along the boulevard, the wind is gusting
The trees, they are dancing in the wind

These dreams of these, So genuine, so true

Sauntering along the city sidewalks
We are talking, we are laughing
Sometimes just the gift, of each others presence
Just knowing that each other is there

These dreams of these, so genuine, so true

Candlelight dinners
Sitting close by fireside

These dreams of these
So genuine, so true

Peter B. LeBuhn

Thoughts of you wrap around my soul

Thoughts of you wrap around my soul
With you on my mind
losing control
Subdued by your passion
Conquered by your charms
Melting in your arms
...Thoughts of you wrap around my soul
This love has set off fire alarms
Wanting to hold back
But forth ventured
into the sexual unknown
This love we shall not postpone
Rushing in...like a tornado
A climatic zone
...Thoughts of you wrap around my soul
Wrapped around my soul
These thoughts will live
Forever

Peter LeBuhn

TIMELESS

The hour is timeless
Still
Caught in a moment
A fire has been lit to the wick
of our Passions.
Our hearts smoldering with each smile
Each glance
The heat...It does increase
Our hearts cannot part
The fire is ablaze.
Caught up now in each others arms
The world outside does not matter
Engulfed in Each others Passions
Drenched in Each others Love
A Timeless Treasure we are living
A gift of each other to each other

Peter B LeBuhn

TO SERVE

Not to swerve
To strive
For the Most High
Not to Yield
My faith...Is my shield
Your ways...My ways
For my Father
The Distance I will go
I will Follow
You are at my side when I feel
Hollow
To succeed is not of my doing
It is full faith in the Father
That Guides Me
Through My Life
Father you have released me from
My strife
You have released me from my strife

Peter LeBuhn

TO THE WHITE SEA

The journey is made
Being drawn nearer
Life choices become clearer

Feet sinking in the white sands
The moon and the stars
Looking down
Speaks volumes in the quietness of my heart
The roar of the tide
Opens up my mind

What Stylist? What Genius?
Painted a land such as this.
Alone in the eyes of my maker
Humbled
Feeling Small
In Awe
Of this great gift He has given me
Most of All

Peter LeBuhn

TRANSPORT TO ECSTASY

Grabbing, Stroking, Sucking Moaning
On Transport to ecstasy
sensual utterance in the night.
Taken by surprise
in the middle of the night
Out of our bodies
Our desires to flight 101 lusty flight.

Kitchen, hallway, Dining Room Table
Living Room, Stairwell, You strip me naked there
In the boudoir all hott, whet and full of passion
nothing could be better...

anywhere you take me
Ready for your action.

Melting kisses, knowing hands
and probing fingertips
transporting you to desire
as your flowers lips are spread.

Indescribable sensations
when you touch my bodies heat
My phallic treasure enters
making us complete.

Do you feel the HEAT
Do you feel the HEAT

SSSSSSSSSSSSSSSSSS
HOTTTTT
Peter LeBuhn

UN BESO EPICO(A SPANISH CROSSOVER SONG)

Un Beso Épico

(An Epic Kiss)

Desamparado en su rapsodia

(Helpless in your rhapsody)

El descubrimiento dulce encontró

(The sweet discovery found)

Bajo su cuerpo

(Under your body)

Perdido en su abismo

(Lost in your abyss)

Perdido en sus brazos... sus piernas envueltas alrededor de thee

(Lost in your arms...Your legs wrapped around thee)

No hay lugar que estaría algo.

(There is no place I would rather be.)

El gotear en sudor apasionado

(Dripping in Passionate Sweat)

el atontamiento es su silueta.

(stunning is your silhouette.)

el osculating, acariciando

(osculating, caressing)

Nuestro amor que confiesa.

(Our love confessing.)

' Neath la luna

('Neath the Moon)

Las Estrellas

(The Stars)

Solamente en naturaleza... es los nuestros.

(Alone in Nature...It is Ours.)

Para ver su resplandor

(To see your glow)

Demuestra

(It does show)

Su felicidad

(Your happiness)

Como usted pone en mina se arma.

(As you lay in mine arms.)

Usted fijó de mis alarmar sexuales.

(You set off my sexual alarms.)

Tomado Más arriba

(Taken Higher)

El cuerpo de Thy fijó sexual en el fuego

(Thy Body Sexually set on Fire)

Mi corazón llameante y despertado

(My heart flaming and aroused)

Como usted se presenta con la invitación sexual.

(As you present yourself with sexual invitation.)

Su sabor dulce del sabor... I

(Your sweet flavour...I savour)

Olor del chocolate de las fresas...

(Smell of Strawberries...Chocolate)

Dentro de su cuerpo colombiano marrón profundo

(Inside your deep brown colombian body)

El Palpitar, Pulsando

(Throbbing, Pulsating)

Rítmico En Amor

(Rhythmical In Love)

... usted tiene thee con su beso épico

(...You Have thee with your Epic Kiss)

... Su Beso Épico

(...Your Epic Kiss)

Peter LeBuhn

UNBRIDLED LOVE

Gliding jasmine oil over sensitive flesh.
Your softness... long silky hair caressing a naked back.
Your taste of sweetness and honey on a blushing nipple.
Thy sharp nibble on your neck
as you throw back your head
The coldness of ice on pleasure warmed skin.
Teasing you with thine feather over trembling shaking thighs.
Warm wetness of your lips as I drink of your nectar
Unbridled Love
At our Fingertips
We Give one another.
... everywhere.

2006 Peter B. Lebuhn

WAITING

Waiting
dressed as a lady in waiting
You come unto me
In the mist of the night
The river so bright
The moon shines above
smiling on the stars
The tide roars in
almost speaking in voice
On the sand
You approach
Through a cloud of fog
First your legs
Then your arms as they swing
Followed by your glorious body
with a mysterious smile

You come upon me not stopping

We are engulfed

The TWO...ONE

Waiting No more

Peter LeBuhn

WE WILL LOVE AGAIN

Sitting in bed, my lamp light out
My head spins from the days doubts
My body is hot feeling the ache in that one special spot
No one to hold, no one to sooth as I sleep
Going on underfoot
My dreams coming alive
Coming upon a sweet flower
She undresses me slowly
Dark hair and light eyes
The perfect woman, nothing to hide
Giving me what I need
My wants
Licking my lips, egging her on
Hips thrust, cloths strewn
Feeling her tongue deep on my manhood
Now laying down
Fully exposed
Perfection magnificent too much for this large buck
Working my way forward
Taking her in
Her awaiting lips part in passion

licking the tips of my penis
Kissing my stomacher
Moaning in sexual want
Pushing her off
Taking her in my arms and thrusting into me
Together into my arms and thrusting into me
Together we come
Two lovers fighting in a battle
Then it's all over
Back in the nights shadows
Again We will love again
Again we will love again.

Peter LeBuhn

When Night Becomes Day

When Night Becomes Day
When Darkness Turns to Light
The Cold Wind concedes to the Warmth
The Passion...The Heat...The Affection
...Rises
...When Night Becomes Day
Two worlds collide
A soiree of emotion
Pours into a bottomless Love potion
...When Night Becomes Day
The coolness of the Night
Cool breeze against our Naked Hide.
Embraced under a moonlit Night
Everything to Confide
Deep Inside We know there will be no Divide.
It is now Day... The warmth of the Sun

Beams our Hide...We Smile at each other
No one shall come asunder
When two worlds collide
When Night Becomes Day

Peter LeBuhn

WITHOUT WORD

Dedicated to the woman who has inspired me, she knows who she is.

Without word you left for a far off land
... Without a plan...You Left... I waited and cried for you
What were you going to do?

When the news hit the front page.
... My heart shipwrecked... to the bottom of the sea

Without word
You left for a far off land
... Without a plan
I worried and cried for you
What were you going to do?

I searched the world over
But I found no trace
... Honey where are you hiding your beautiful face

I will be there to ease your pain
I will make you the center of my world
... And maybe make you happy awhile.

Wherever you are in that far off land
... I am with you
... I am with you
We will meet again-I know we will meet again

Peter B. Lebuhn

WONDROUS LIFE

What a wondrous life is this I lead
From my heart love does bleed
...My life I live for thee
...My love I give to thee

My Garden of fruitful mystery
and splendor
You will enter

You take me by the hand
Around each corner
....A new surprise
....To Find

What a wondrous life is this I lead
From my heart love does bleed
Peter LeBuhn

Peter LeBuhn

YOUR GOLDEN KISS

Your Golden Kiss
Calling to my heartstrings
What is to be made of this?
You play me like a love instrument
In Concert with your every desire
The love we make is lyrical, musical
Playing the strings every so softly
Ever so slightly playing louder, stronger
Enter the Brass...The percussion
Your kind of love
Nearly gives me a concussion.
In your arms
Before thee
Naked, Bare, Whet and Raw
This love keeps going
No sign of a stall.
You take me...make me
Yours
Your dinner plate
for you to explore.
A pleasure plate for your taste.

Lying Bare in the Sand
Trembling
Not to Withstand
You Kiss me With your Eyes
I Kiss you with mine.
Not a word spoken
We smile at each other
Much is said in silence
Our silence says I love you
Thanks to Your Golden Kiss
Your Golden Kiss
Peter LeBuhn

TOUCH ME THERE

Touch Me There...

You're always there,
in my dreams,
and I'm wonderfully weak,
savoring each
of your moist kisses.
My desire only heightens
as your lips press
against every inch
of my flesh...
except for that
one spot,
which I won't
tell you about now.
And I only ask
that you'll touch me
there later.

YOUR TOUCH MEANS SO MUCH

Looking into Your Eyes
Feeling Love gushing throughout my heart
At first glance
I know you are the one.
In my heart, Is this intense passion or emotion?
Now Knowing this love is genuine

Your touch means so much
Won't you come hug me
Won't you come love me

Come along with me
We will run hand in hand In fields so green.
We share precious moments together
We lay by the fire in the winter
We hold each close

Your touch means so much
Won't you come hug me
Won't you come love me

Your sensitivity fills me with joy when I am down
You are like a princess who wears a crown
Life is so much more wonderful while you are in my world
From all this you must be able to tell
I love you

Your touch means so much
Won't you come hug me
Won't you come love me

Peter LeBuhn